S

'A graceful, refreshingly wise and grounding collage of life, death, loss, other-life, myth, nature and invention. These infinite themes are uniquely handled and dexterously narrated by Haskell. *Stroking Cerberus* is a stunning, original debut collection that encourages contemplation as much as it motivates the reader to explore and review where separations occur and opposites coalesce. This is a timely, intimate, but far-reaching narrative, and a necessary joy to get to know.'

—Jane Monson

Jacqueline
Haskell

STROKING
CERBERUS

POEMS FROM THE AFTERLIFE

First published in 2020 by
Myriad Editions
www.myriadeditions.com

Myriad Editions
An imprint of New Internationalist Publications
The Old Music Hall, 106–108 Cowley Rd,
Oxford OX4 1JE

First printing
1 3 5 7 9 10 8 6 4 2

A CIP catalogue record for this book
is available from the British Library

ISBN (pbk): 978-1-912408-46-7
ISBN (ebk): 978-1-912408-47-4

Designed by WatchWord Editorial Services, London
Typeset in Dante by www.twenty-sixletters.com

Printed and bound in Great Britain
by CPI Group (UK) Ltd, Croydon CR0 4YY

To our beautiful boy,
who was nothing like Cerberus.

Matt Lawson
24th March 2003—9th July 2019

Contents

Static

*In 1939, American photographer Attila von Szalay experimented
with a phonograph record cutter to capture spirit voices;
in later years, he used a wire recorder.*

What's it like behind a waning moon?
Is there anybody there with you?

The dog—is he there too?
I admit it, I'm a little anxious now—
he always loved
    you more than me—
please say he is.

*(You leave a gap in case they answer,
then, as instructed, you play it backwards,
the tape, again and again.)*

(Nothing but the empty wire, again and again.)

(You creep up on it, hope to catch it spooling.)

(Nothing but the empty wire.)

(Nothing.)

1

White Noise

In the October 1920 issue of the American Magazine,
*Thomas Alva Edison revealed that he was developing
an electrical device—to speak with the dead.*

yellow, pink,
artefacts of silence, all
discarnates of the airwaves;
the flim-flam of your thirsty goblin smile
through glass and rain
and mirrored
extra-terrestrial miles
at 1485 KHz (the famed Jürgenson Frequency)
I scry for you, in the ether

The Binary of the Dead

*In 1940s Grosseto, Italy, Marcello Bacci claimed
to be able to pick up the voices of the deceased
on a vacuum tube radio; sometimes
these whisperings were accompanied
by unexplained tapping.*

the concrete cracks with the *staccato* motions
of your hidden code

11001110:10101001

dot dot dot dash dash dash dot dot dot

your alarm call reaches me,
reminding me, how
your dead are never quite your dead

Layerings

You drift back from it. The found pennies,
money for fares and crossings, fluff mossing from
    pocket to pocket,
old Elastoplasts heavy with blood and perfume.
    Mrs Dalloway,
so despised in life; inside the cover a scribbled
    shopping list—
no *two*—and underneath, a water-damaged box,
    not opened since.

You lean back from it. The wall behind you crusty
with layers of painted-over cabbage roses, pale
    as river ice.
Greasy vermilion splotches adorn her dresser top,
charting *my Vivienne Westwood phase, darling*,
as she called it; lips pursed for
    Peachy Mama; Occult Red; Brouhaha.

In the hallway, magnolia gives way to random
shades of pink—what *was* she thinking?—
each coat not quite covering the last.

You go to throw it out, that damaged box—
    just champagne glasses
and the breath of past lips fogging wide,
    shallow rims,
gold trim fading with the Christmas light.

But at the bottom, a snapshot taken with an old
    Brownie by your brother,
you in his bed: too-big pyjamas, flannelette sheets,
hot water bottles, the promise of Rich Tea
    and milk if you don't disturb.

You hear her still, your mother, heels tick-tocking
    towards you
across the parquet flooring, and *auldlangsyne*
    comes early,
the midnight rising, each New Year emulsioned over,
not quite covering the last.

Peachy Mama

It touched your skin.

The last thing it knew was you,
your faulty DNA smeared on its stubby tip.

I ache to extract your code from its shine,
rebuild you cell by cell,

cover your face in loose-powder kisses,
tell you it always suited you, this colour.

And I, whom it does not suit,
I can wear no other.

My Father's Hands

To my own father, who served on Flower-class corvettes,
employed during WW2 as anti-submarine convoy escorts,
during the Battle of the Atlantic.

My father's hands
are wide and strong
their knuckles boot-black hairy
nails filed soft
beyond the quick
and the albatross flight

hands that command
their ship deep
in the north-Atlantic
straight and true from Tobermoray
out of Holy Loch and the Cloch
Point light

from the blind-ice of
the fiddler's storm
to the sea wolves
whistling in their lair
superstitious as crossed knives
or women on the lee

the waves all sauced up
currents opening wide to
let the convoy through
food and medicine
to the Republic in
the Spanish War

and in the after-years
an inset diamond
a square gold ring
materialises—*an admirer*
from before your mother—
now removed by me, his

daughter, with a spit
of soap and water
from those hands
that set their course without me
crossed on his chest
like two knives out at sea

Unexpected Contact

We read over the instructions.

Sit knee to knee. Face the board.
Lady and Gentleman preferred.
Hold the planchette—and
each other—lightly.
Start easy. Be prepared for unexpected contact.

Nothing moves: our fingers, the planchette. Nothing.

We hear what sounds like a radio—a TV even—
out there, in the ether (oh, how we miss TV!).
A theme tune: *Coronation Street…*

> Did she die, Ena Sharples? Did she?
> Yes, *this* is what we need to know!

Don't be too hard on them
if they don't come through first time, it says,
they are busy people, the living.

Relying on the Dead for Company

It never works—they've seen too much of life,
    think themselves superior.

Still, you leave a gap in case they answer,
    then, as instructed,
you play it backwards, the empty tape, the wire…

(the tape, the wire, again and again)

(the tape, the wire)

(the tape)

Finally, you realise there is little in it between
this world and the other; you become acquainted
with the silence.

Do I know you?
I hope so.
I do hope so.

RSVP

Balloon Child

A balloon child, formed of air
and water, no substance at all.

A dandelion clock inside me,
a helium laugh,
a phantom moon
of pregnancies, old and new.

A silver charm from another life,
a christening shoe,
a puff of pressure, a Doppler scan
deflating.

Inside me, my balloon child,
still, and borrowed, and blue.

Amelie

Honeycombed you keep me here,
with her lunch box
and whatever else it is you, her father,
think she might still need.

What about her room, her things? I ask him.

Papier-mâché insects swarm her windowsill,
bright ladybugs fly home across the wallpaper,
an old doll sprawls on a chair,
its eyelids drooping.

Oh, we'll keep them...

And her hair?

Her hair pressed into the pages of the order of
    service,
stranded between the *Miserere mei* and the
    Deus salutis meae,
braids tight as summer keys,
unused and chlorinating in their locks;
the empty changing rooms, the hum of the pool filter.

Mummy, Mummy, it sounds like singing bees!

The crumbling heat of cement walls, the torn frill
from last year's swimsuit,
the crack of her skull on mermaid tiles,
the splash of a silkie's fin,

and our lapse, our one,
single lapse
our cavern,

a lacuna,

her body
billowing underwater.

13

Dark Feathers

(In which you hire a demon hunter)

And the colour of the sky, on your planet? He asks me.
Green, I say, without hesitation,
gazing at the underside of a passing bird,
belly looping on the wing
(always a habit of mine, this inversion).

A camera obscura. *Crazy me!*—I think the pool a sea.

Keep away from the pool! He tells me.
Demons travel easily through a body of water.

Voices, yes, voices,
skim its surface,
ghosts for waves…

Beneath me, I can hear it sucking, this inversion.
Ripples dancing like a shoal of tiny silver fish;
I can hear it, the whispering of the pool filter,
streaks of phosphorescence raking
dark feathers from its line.

Cora

Before the topcoat dries and the last joists are
    pinned,
she has lost heart, the new made old before it is
    begun,
in this, the land of the old, *his* old,

the land of great-aunts and antimacassars,
of sedge and sallow, reed birds in flight on
    ridgelines
where she's a woman alone with a half-done house
    and farm,

and outside the workmen quarrelling, the riptide
    breaking, rising,
the fields, stretching ahead, hedgerows, their
    corners dark with mossy sod;
above the house, the quarry—yes, even the quarry,
    with its white cliffs and narrow cuts—

even the quarry imprisons her, thins her, whitens
    her until…

…he drifts back into her dream, the-same-but-always
     dream,
where he comes on foot, calls to her through water,
     his Cora,

stepping out across the sands of the bay, her diver,
passing through her, her webbed diver back from the
     deep,
silver fish jumping against her, worming inside her

as she wades towards the porpoise and the seals and
     the kittiwakes,
past the ghostly Finnbar in his borrowed longboat,
     struggling
with the three dipping lug sails that will one day
     sink him

until she's but a speck in her own red sail of a dress,
     skirts gathered,
tucked into navy knickers, as when she was a child.

Rockies

I'm so close I can
almost hear you breathing.

My hands graze the padded shoulder of your jacket—
you brush me off like dandruff;
for one soft, blind moment your fingers cool on mine.

You peer out into that poor and stunted light,
that December-afternoon dark,
and for an instant—a marvellous, fantastical instant—
I think you see me, my headscarf with the red checks,
my carefully drawn emaciation,
then you turn away,
indifferent to your own reflection.

Ah, but when you sleep! When you sleep,
I take you to the Rockies of your childhood
—Boulder Pass and Ptarmigan—lakes glossy as
    river glass,
stepping out into the Fish Creek parking lot,
all shrimp net and flowered wellingtons,

and we chip away at them, those boulders,
until I'm your mother, and you, you are my child again.

Wild Goose Song

Outside,
an immaculate formation
a perfect apostrophe of grace
fills the windscreen of our plane

the *caw caw* of seven silver cursors in the sky

then the snap and cackle of engine one

the smell of burning birds
blistered and browned
these sundog carrion.

Inside,
goose slaughter
an intake of feathered breath

the sharp pop and crackle of engine two
as geese and plane glide together in cathedral silence.

Below us, the icy Hudson parts,
a rimose welcome
for an old grey whale
returning to its master.

Isthmus

Can you see me? I ask you,

  because earlier,
  down by Hells Cliff where
  the samphire grows and the
tide swims with shells,
  the dog ran out of the waves,
  rounding by the rock
pools and the dark lighthouse,
  a sand-crab in his teeth,

  and he couldn't find
  me—I could
  see him searching—
  though I was right there, where
   he'd left me—I could
  see him looking—
right at me
through me

    as I stopped collecting
      the mussels (half-
  wrenched from their beardy beds)
      and the dog

                                        barked,
                    a strangled salt-water sound,
                    frenzied
                    by my absence.

Can you see me? I ask you,

                    a strand of silver seaweed curling
                    between my fingers,
        me naked on your plate, your fork
                    pressing into
                    the angel-flesh   of my body,
                    bacon curing, the samphire shrinking
                                        away from me
                                                in the pan.

You're not *present*, Evie,

                    you can't even eat with me,
        you say,
                    pushing the rind and a splinter
                    from the scrambled black-headed
                    gull's egg
                                to the side of your plate,
                                where
        you

lay down
your knife,
your fork,
pick a strand of something silver
from your teeth,
collect your keys from the sideboard.

When you are gone,

I pick up that rind,
breathe you
in

you,
your arms salty, your heart crusted,
your belly, too;

I take a bite of you,
then another.

The Carrying

The men came for you,
eyes bloody, whites exposed
in the carrying of you;

the groaning of it,
the turning of you
at the steep angle of the path;

its zigzag of gorse and sheep,
yellow flowers and caught wool,
frothy as the bay.

And your wicker box greening, swelling.
Inside, your feet bound,
your skin sliding back on bones.

Below you, the white birds crying,
the oily sea waiting,
and the pushing off,

the hissing of the pebbles,
the pull strong, stronger
than the rut of deer.

When they are gone
I search for you—the back field, the bothy—
then finally, I cave in to night,

thimble and quilt fading in my lap.
The kerosene spluttering, just the once:
a sudden draught under the door

and you are here behind me,
loosening my black ribbon,
drawing down my hair in your hands,

your fingers webbed, translucent,
knuckles shimmering,
skin stained by the tide.

Passing Place

i.

Your front tyre punctures and we dismount,
walk another mile in the lee of weathered pines,
white birds cawing high against the sea.

Beneath us, the path sinks to a single track,
our bikes scraping the fence,
beach bags irritating mosquito legs.

Then suddenly, the passing place appears,
and so, we stop. You kneel before me,
head bowed, hands gentle on the wheel.

Later, I think perhaps we shall wade out,
catch sand-crabs, pick samphire, but
when it comes to it,

you—ever the hunter—
hold out the net to me, its mesh
glistening, empty.

ii.

Sometimes, I sniff the cones for memories of that
    beach,
but there's just the slightest tang of empty-suitcase
    leather—
it seems, like you, they do not travel well.

Though, apparently, you can tell the weather
    by them—
their woody, splintered selves
the curved edges of a window-ledge barometer.

Open fair; closed for rain.

iii.

I hold one to my ear and think I hear some thready
    inner wisps of you,
you, with your hunter bones bleached high and white
    by the tide,

your lips pale and bitter as the moon, my skin
    pressing into you,
my body open, my fingers curling on the clinic's
    flannel bedsheet,

one hand fearing rain.

East Stour

Not long after, I spot you in the wildflower fields,
pale limbs bone-thin, rice-raw,
your face singed with dew,
everywhere the reek of gillyflowers and sorrel.

And the poppy-flame of your shadow
makes me want to follow you,
you, with your lamb knuckles,
white with fleece and spring.

Three Days You Were Gone

It was…*unexpected*, shall we say…

not that you came back, but that you should be gone
    at all.
We never asked, though we couldn't help but wonder;
in truth, we were a little in awe of you, a little afraid,
    back then,
and of course, you never told us.

Some other life than this, was all you said, when
    pressed,
spoken between mouthfuls of cinnamon toast and
    eggs
as we sat you down at the table, tea already brewed,
bitter, dark, smoky, in the pot.

After you'd eaten, you insisted we cross the marsh
    without you,
everyone heads down and collars up—much the same
    as usual—
hounds running before us in the wind.

And so, we left you there, alone in your workshop,
your hands freshly sutured from
    the tearing of nails on skin,
greeting your beloved rosewood plane, barely able to
    hold it—

or so we thought.

We found you then, the shavings fresh from the cross
    you'd fashioned—
had been making all this time—with your own
    hands...
our own nails, for God's sake. You'd even cut grass,
hidden greenery for the camels.
Gifts of our own private wilderness.

Another life and *just in case*, was all you said,
in the letter that you left us: in case
they should release you, *in case it comes to this*—
as if you'd known it would.

We found you, the one wrist nailed,
the one foot gouged, still slippery and anointed,
the broken alabaster pooling with oil, your body
    hanging,
hair tangled and thorned and bloodied through,
your hand an outstretched hammer falling.

Self-raising

Weeks on, your shopping sits there on the counter:
green lentils, chickpeas, parchment-wrapped herbs,
sage and lovage tied with string.

Finally, I decide to tidy you away.
I open the larder cupboard and out fly cornflakes
 —*What the fuck?*—then buckwheat
(two pounds, opened), almond flour and quinoa;
a plastic container strikes me just above the
     eyebrow,
hurls itself at the kitchen units, its lid popping
     oatmeal bran,
scattering an ash of silver dust across the lino.

I slam my weight against the door, but *whoosh!*
some unseen force defies me, snaps it
back on its hinges, and I'm ragdolled against those
     units
—dark blue, glossy, retro; so *kitsch*, you once said—
a thin ant-trail of blood marching through my eye.

That night, I restore order, leave porridge oats
to quietly sow their seeds; cupboards crammed
with gluten-free, empty of forgiveness.

Not yet knowing that one day, one day, you will speak
    to me again,
so softly I'll mistake it for the hiss of summer rain.

That Great Artificer

Without warning: high tide.
There is no time,
just the waters
rising, grains circling

dreams of his son's salvation;
Icarus, that shadow-life,
where dark feathers alight soft
upon a waxing moon.

White sea; stone Labyrinth.
He cleaves the path
behind him, silt gyrating
in its quick.

Sleight of sand, Daedalus
is his own creation,
goading Minos to its
very centre.

The Acheron

She tells him she needs a witness
to the murmurings of the Shades
in that cataclysmic place,
lest in the drinking of the Lethe
she forgets.

He agrees to go with her, names his price.
He clambers from his skiff, makes fast his pole
and chalks a rudimentary sign:

Self-hire—outbound only.

Honesty Box:

> *No foreign coins.*
> *No change given.*

ferryman

turning back mid-tide
I thought you knew the way? he said

Down and Out in the Upper World

He takes her money, of course he does,
walks in a world he's never seen but soon despises.

There is no work here for the likes of him.
He has no transferable skills. No CV.

He finds a blanket in the underpass and settles down
with the shells of men who would not

pay his fee. He dreams of a great darkness, of a river,
viscid, burning, full of deviant attractions.

He keeps his money close to his chest;
he has no idea how things work here.

They take his money, of course they do,
those men who need it for fares and crossings.

They go to clasp his hands, seal his lips,
amorous in their corruptibility.

Blue

the house is to be sold complete with bluebell wood,
lying due west between the Nine Springs
and the White Tor, seventeen acres
all told, by private treaty

We were lonely childhood scholars then,
stepping through that mine of fecund
    bluebells,
pollen-dusted, pushing through garlic,
    wood anemones,
    celandine,
their shadows dark and still.

We read—so says Ovid—of how Apollo made
    a flower with his tears,
lamenting the shed blood of the dying prince
    Hyakinthos. *Ai, ai,*
the wail of mourning stained the new-formed
petals, turning them inside out
    with grief.

You would have made light of such blues,
that small part of you, that Dorian god,

who lived and died with the seasons of the wood,
like the bluebells that came and went in a blink of
    pale stars.

In what was the formal garden, now I hide-and-seek
    you,
our rope-and-bucket swing, our finger chains, no
    trace
—but, Oh! Here! One rotting lime-green thread of
    you,
with chocolate stripes—*our mother's knitting!*

and the air bursting forth with the fizz
of two Love Hearts melting, held beneath
our tongues like communion wafers
Kiss me   True love   Be mine

Walking in our wood—what is left of our wood—
our gleaming wild wild ghost of a wood—
manured fields encroach upon it,
dams call away the water from its stream, and
    suddenly
suddenly I am washed by the sound and the sea of
    you,

the smell and the thread of you,
the lime-green and the chocolate of you,
by garlic as crushed and wild and past as you.

Back in the Great Hall my signature dawdles
on the vellum of the notary's lonely final page;
I sign away the house, *ai, ai,* my mark, *ai, ai,*
an Orpheus in his Upper World.

Orpheus

He does not look back.

In time, she resents this.
They bicker.
He is cruel.
She asks him to move out.

She finds she craves it, the Underworld—
the light here hurts her eyes.
The days are too long, and she misses the dog.
Let me in, she pleads, fisting the gates, *let me in!*

But they will not.

That night, she hears the shadow-howl of Cerberus,
strokes his heads as he lays them on her pillow,
feels his hot breath at her neck,
and returns to the cavern of her dreams.

Motherdaughter

i.

In the day room, where she swears she's never been,
tabled condiments line up as invading armies on the
    march.

15, 16, 17, she counts them, voice hoarse from
    repetition,
then turns away—*Coming, ready or not!* she cries.

Is this a game? She can't (coming where?)
remember (ready for what?), but hides herself away,
    just in case.

I've seen the shadow of my death, she says to no one in
    particular,
when they find her, squatting behind the curtains.

ii.

A nurse calls you. *We've had something of an issue
    with Fiona.*
(Your mother's name is Finoula. They know this—

she's been there six years.) When you arrive, you find
    her in the day room,
kneeling. Plucking threadbare cabbage roses

from the carpet, scratching at the pile,
    nails torn
and bleeding at the quick. You kneel with her,

your face inches from hers. A grande dame,
she pulls herself up: *These roses*, she whispers,
    need water.

Shell

The twentieth century English occultist Aleister Crowley
refers to 'ghosts' as the 'Shells of the Dead', where the
'Shell' is what is left behind by a Spirit after it has
reincarnated, and its appearance on Earth
is what we might call a 'haunting'.

They follow me, the locusts,
across the dirty roses
of the dining room carpet.
The room itself is oddly bare,
missing its table, curtains, chairs;
only the aspidistra remains,
and her cane, of course, her cane.

My mother, Janus-faced,
suddenly here in front of me,
eating cake through a veil.
What have they done to you, Mother,
in this afterlife of yours,
that you need to shield your face?

And those locusts, an upsurge,
devouring her hand, the cake—
shapeshifters all.

It is in this *not* seeing,
this absorption in the void,
that I see her
as I never did in life.

Visual Purple

Of what am I afraid?

Of still being in my pyjamas at ten.
Of picnics left untouched.

That there is nothing out there.
That there is everything out there.

Tell me something I couldn't possibly know.

Can you see it?

See what?

The noise of passing clouds, the smell of flowers fading.

Of course, of course, I mumble, but where?

A firefly masquerading as an aura orb,
washing skipping in an unexpected gust of ectoplasm,
rose petals falling at my feet.

All and none of this I see.

Do you remember? I say.

Remember what, my lovely lovely?

Oh, please! (Even in life you were a charmer.)

Remember what?

On the lens of your eye, as you passed over,
the last thing you saw was me.

Notes on the text

Balloon Child

Spiritualists offer up 'beyond the veil' explanations when a pregnancy ends in loss, looking at it as part of the endless pattern of life being an exchange, rather than as a singular event.

Wild Goose Song

On 15 January 2009, US Airways flight 1549 struck a flock of Canada geese on the climbout from NYC's LaGuardia Airport, losing all engine power and ditching in the Hudson River. All passengers and crew were rescued.

That Great Artificer

Daedalus built the Labyrinth for King Minos of Crete, who imprisoned his enemies there to be killed by the mythical monster the Minotaur. However, King Minos became angry with Daedalus for advising Princess Ariadne to give Theseus the thread that helped him escape the Labyrinth after killing the Minotaur, and he had Daedalus and his son, Icarus, imprisoned inside it. Daedalus devised a plan to escape the Labyrinth on wings made of wax. They escaped, but Icarus flew too close to the sun, the wax melted and he fell to his death.

The Acheron

In ancient Greek mythology, the Acheron was one of the five rivers of the Underworld, and was known as 'the river of woe'. Charon ferried the dead across the Acheron to transport them from the Upper to the Lower World.

Visual Purple

Inspired by Franz Christian Boll's discovery of rhodopsin—or 'visual purple', a photosensitive pigment present in the rods of the retina—German physiologist Wilhelm Kühne discovered that the rhodopsin could be 'imprinted' like a photographic negative. This led to a belief in the early twentieth century that the retina of the eye recorded the last image seen before death.

Original sources

'Amelie' was Highly Commended in the Fish Poetry Competition 2014, and was published in the *Fish Anthology 2014*, July 2014

'Blue' was published in the *High Window* quarterly review of poetry, #8, December 2017

'Cora' won second prize in the Canterbury Festival Poet of the Year Competition 2015, and was published in the *Canterbury Festival Poet of the Year* anthology, October 2015

'Dies Infaustus' (now titled 'My Father's Hands') won second prize in the Sherborne Literary Festival Open Poetry Competition 2014

'Three' (an earlier version of 'Three Days You Were Gone') was published in *Anomaly Literary Journal: Issue 2*, March 2016

'Wild Goose Song' was performed at Greenwich Theatre by Live Canon, and published in *Emerging Poets*, October 2009

Acknowledgements

Particular thanks go to: Matt Freidson, deputy director at Creative Future, for his endless encouragement; Candida Lacey, publishing director at Myriad, for getting this manuscript into your hands so efficiently, and Victoria Heath Silk, editor, for so brilliantly shoehorning my rambling stanzas into this pocket edition; Emma Seal, for taking such a fab author photo of me; Helena Nelson at Happen*Stance* for such generous use of her reading windows; New Writing South who found Maria Jastrzębska, my Spotlight mentor—thank you, Maria, for attempting to teach me everything you know in just eight hours; Elżbieta Wójcik-Leese, my amazing Poetry School teacher and friend; Giles Darvill, for reading early drafts with such grace and humour over the dinner table; and Michael Forester, writer, for allowing me a glimpse of his poetic life.

About the author

Jacqueline Haskell is a deaf poet and novelist. She has an MA in Creative Writing from Birkbeck, and her debut novel, *The Auspice*, was a finalist in the 2018 Bath Novel Award. Her short fiction has been listed in many competitions, including the Bridport Prize and the Asham Award.

About Spotlight

Spotlight Books is a collaboration between Myriad Editions, Creative Future and New Writing South to discover, guide and support writers whose voices are under-represented.

Our aim is to spotlight new talent that otherwise would not be recognised, and to help writers who face barriers, or lack opportunities, to develop their creative and professional skills in order to create a lasting legacy of work.

Each of our three organisations is dedicated to specific aspects of writer development. Together we are able to offer a clear ladder of support, from mentorship through to development editing and promotional opportunities.

Spotlight books are not only treasures in themselves but also beacons to other under-represented writers. For further information, please visit: www.creativefuture.org.uk

Spotlight is supported by Arts Council England.

'These works are both nourishing and inspiring, and a gift to any reader.'—Kerry Hudson

Spotlight stories

Georgina Aboud
Cora Vincent

Tara Gould
The Haunting of Strawberry Water

Ana Tewson-Božić
Crumbs

Spotlight poetry

Jacqueline Haskell
Stroking Cerberus: Poems from the Afterlife

Elizabeth Ridout
Summon

Sarah Windebank
Memories of a Swedish Grandmother